Christmas is Jesus' birthday, you know.
And our families worship baby Jesus
at Christmastime, just like YOU do!

Editor: Diane Stortz
Designer: Coleen Davis

The Standard Publishing Company, Cincinnati, Ohio
A division of Standex International Corporation
Text © 1993 by Susan Titus Osborn and Christine Harder Tangvald
Illustrations © 1993 by The Standard Publishing Company
Printed in the United States of America
00 99 98 97 96 95 94 93   5 4 3 2 1

Library of Congress Catalog Card Number 93-6683
ISBN 0-87403-799-9
Cataloging-in-Publication data available

Children Around The World CELEBRATE CHRISTMAS!

Susan Titus Osborn and Christine Tangvald
illustrated by Jodie McCallum

STANDARD PUBLISHING
Cincinnati, Ohio

Hi!
Merry Christmas from **CHINA!**
My name is **Yen-chi** (YEN-shee).
What is *your* name?

I live on a boat called a *sampan* on the Whangpoo River,
near the HUGE city of Shanghai in the country of China.

I have a sister named Shu-ying (SHOO-ying) and a
brother named Tien-min (TEN-men). We love to fish from
our boat, and we can jump right off the side to go
SWIMMING! Don't you wish you could swim right off
your front porch?

One of my *favorite* things to do at Christmastime is to make a paper CHRISTMAS LANTERN. Very carefully, my dad cuts out three wise men and puts them on a circle inside the lantern. When we light the red candle, the wise men move in a circle — following the star, looking for BABY JESUS! I love to watch the wise men go around and around and around.

We celebrate the Chinese New Year at the same time we celebrate Christmas. My mom makes yummy candy from rice flour and sugar. We set off lots of *fireworks* —
bright colored fountains
gold and silver sparklers
and (my favorites) the SKY ROCKETS!

The way we say "Merry Christmas" in Chinese is
"Kung Hei Shing Taan."
(goong-hoh-sheng-tahn)
Can you say *that?*

If you ever come to China, maybe you can go swimming with us! But you will have to watch out for Tien-min — he might splash you! He splashes *everybody!*

Good-bye and Merry Christmas
from your friend Yen-chi
in **CHINA!**

Hi!
Merry Christmas from **RUSSIA!**
My name is **Natasha.**
I live in the city of Moscow in the country of Russia.

Have you ever gone sledding? In the winter, we have lots
and lots of powdery snow, and the sledding is GREAT!

I have a little brother named Fedya (FEED-yah). He thinks
he is a bear! He likes to hide behind a pine tree, growl like
a bear, and throw snowballs at my friends and me!
I wish he'd STOP!

I love Christmas in Russia!
My favorite thing to do at Christmastime is to dress up like
a *beautiful granddaughter* from the forest. This year I will
wear a sparkling blue dress with snowflakes on the cuffs
and hem.

Isn't it GORGEOUS?

Fedya will dress up like an animal from the forest.
He's going to be (you guessed it!) . . . a BEAR!

On Christmas Eve we eat delicious egg rolls with beef, pork, and bear meat inside. (Yum, yum!) Then we decorate the Christmas tree. I made some paper dolls to hang on the tree this year.

Guess what Fedya made?
Bears, *bears,* and more BEARS!

The way we say "Merry Christmas" in Russian is
"S'Rozhdestvom Khristovym."
(z'roh-DESHT-vohm KRIS-too-vim)
That's hard even for *me* to say!

I'd better go now. I'm supposed to be watching Fedya. He's hiding again, but I can hear him growling like a bear!

Merry Christmas from your friend Natasha
in **RUSSIA!**

Hi!
Merry Christmas from **MEXICO!**
My name is **Pablo.**
I live in the desert village of Chihuahua (chih-WAH-wah) in the country of Mexico.

I have two sisters, Anita and Maria, and a brother named Juanito. We all love to hike in the desert hills.

It is *hot* here in the desert —
HOT, *hot,* HOT!
Giant *saguaro* (suh-WAR-oh) cactuses grow here. They are tall, with long, long arms and sharp, stickery needles. Sometimes they look like they have funny faces . . . like *this* one.

Christmas is my favorite time in Mexico.
We make a *piñata* (pin-YAH-ta).
A *piñata* is so much fun!
Mama fills it with candy and oranges and peanuts.
Papa hangs it from a tree.

Then, WHACK — SMACK! We take turns swinging at
the *piñata* with a big stick — while we are blindfolded!
When someone hits it *just right,* then SMASH! CRASH!
The candy and fruit and nuts spill *all over* the ground!
We SCRAMBLE to see who can pick up the most. Is that
ever fun! I wish we could do it more than once a year.

If you want to make your own *piñata,*
I will tell you how at the back of this book — OK?

On Christmas Eve, visitors with lighted candles often
stand outside our house, singing Christmas hymns. We
invite them in to eat sweet breads and swing at our *piñata.*

Here is how we say "Merry Christmas" in Spanish.
"Feliz Navidad"
(feh-LEES na-vee-DAHD)
Can *you* say that?

I hope you have fun making your *piñata!*
Merry Christmas and good-bye from your friend Pablo
in **MEXICO!**

Hi!
Merry Christmas from **AFRICA!**
My name is **Kanda** (CAN-duh).
I live in the Congo, near the edge of the jungle.

Do you have wild animals where you live? WE DO!
    We have HUGE elephants
    and lots and lots of chattering monkeys
    and swift, sleek gazelles.

I don't have any brothers or sisters, but I have lots of
friends! One of my friends is a missionary. She teaches
us Christmas songs in English.
    Can you sing "SILENT NIGHT, HOLY NIGHT"?
    I'll bet you can. It's my *favorite* Christmas song!

My friends and I are making special Christmas gifts for
Jesus. I'm making a *drum!* During the offering at church,
we will march around a table and lay our gifts for Jesus
there.

I have an idea! Why don't *you* make a gift for Jesus too!
You could make a dish, or a necklace, or even a crown!

After church, we have a Christmas program.
I get to be an ANGEL this year! The Red Cross gave me
this beautiful soft robe, and my missionary friend made
me these silvery wings. I will look *terrific!*

Can you guess what this means?
"Sikukuu ya Kuzaliwa Kristo"
(see-koo-koo yah koo-zah-lee-wah kree-stow)
That's how we say "Merry Christmas"
in our language, Swahili!

Well, I hope you have fun making your
Christmas gift for Jesus! Merry Christmas
and good-bye from your friend Kanda
in the **CONGO!**

Hi!
Merry Christmas from **SAUDI ARABIA!**
My name is **Samina** (sah-MEE-nuh).
I live on the Western Highlands, in the city of Mecca
in the country of Saudi Arabia.

I have a sister named Bibi (BEE-bee).
Bibi and I like to go exploring. We hunt for smooth stones
on the bank of the Red Sea. Do *you* like to go exploring?

At Christmastime, Bibi and I make a big, beautiful wreath
of golden marigolds to hang on our front door.

My favorite thing to do at Christmastime is to go to a
friend's home and act out the Christmas story with songs.
We can't do this at church, because
     WE DON'T HAVE ANY CHURCHES HERE!
It's *true!* Our government won't allow us to build a church
where we can worship Jesus (can you believe *that!*) so we
have to worship Jesus at home.

On Christmas Eve we hold a ceremony in the courtyard of our house. One of the children reads the Christmas story from an Arabic Bible while the rest of us hold lighted candles.

Then we light a big bonfire of *thorns.* It gets HOT! After the fire is out and the ashes are cold, *everyone jumps* on the ashes three times — one, *two,* THREE — and makes a *wish.* Doesn't that sound like FUN? It *is* fun!

The way we say "Merry Christmas" in Arabic is
"Miladun Said."
(mee-lah-doon sah-yeed)
Can you say that?
Good for you!

I hope you have a very "Miladun Said." Good-bye for now from your friend Samina in **SAUDI ARABIA!**

Hi!

Merry Christmas from **FRANCE!**

My name is **Pierre.**

I live near the sea in the town of Aubagne (oo-BAN-ye) in the country of France.

I love to go swimming in the Mediterranean Sea with my brother, Marcel, and my sister, Suzette. We run and splash through the waves as they *smash* and *crash* on the beach. LOOK OUT! *Here I come!*

Do you like to collect seashells? We do.
We walk barefoot in the sand on the seashore looking for them. Here is a BEAUTIFUL one! Once I found a starfish that was *still alive!* (I put it back into the sea — right away!)

At Christmastime, Marcel, Suzette, and I make clay figures called *santons* (san-TOONS). We use our *santons* to make a wonderful *crèche* (nativity scene) in one corner of our kitchen. It looks like this:

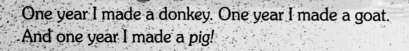

One year I made a donkey. One year I made a goat.
And one year I made a *pig!*

One of the wise men in our *crèche* was broken. So this year when I made my *santon* I surprised my mother with a brand-new wise man. He has a red cape and a white turban and a beautiful golden crown. Now we have three wise men once again!

SAY! Would *you* like to make some *santons* out of clay? I will give you the recipe at the back of this book. Don't forget to make a *santon* of baby JESUS!

Before we go to bed on Christmas Eve, Marcel, Suzette, and I put straw shoes on the hearth by the fire. When we wake up on Christmas morning, they will be filled with toys and candy and nuts. WOW! Look what I got!

Here's how we say "Merry Christmas" in French.

"Joyeaux Noël"

(Zwah-YUH noh-EHL)

Can you say that? Doesn't it sound beautiful?

Well, I hope you have fun making your *santons!* It's been so much fun visiting with you!

Merry Christmas and good-bye for now from your friend Pierre in **FRANCE!**

Hi!

Merry Christmas from **HAWAII!**

My name is **Leilani** (lay-LAWN-ee).

Hawaii is one of the United States of America. I live in Lahaina, near the beach, on the island of Maui in Hawaii.

My brother, Kealii (kaa-a-LEE-ee), and I love to "body surf" on the big waves that roll in toward the beach. You should see us! Have you ever tried to body surf?
It's FUN!

We also like to snorkel on the coral reef where the silver angelfish and the neon gobies swim. But we have to be careful of the green moray eels — *they* can STING!

I love Christmas in Hawaii. One of my favorite things to do at Christmas is to pick big, beautiful bouquets of red poinsettias and white orchids for our house. We even pick some for the grandma who lives next door.

On Christmas Eve, I play my ukulele in the Christmas pageant at church. STRUM — STRUM — STRUM!

After the pageant, we all go down to the beach and have a HUGE Christmas *luau!* (That's a banquet.)

Mmmmmm, GOOD!
We roast a whole pig in a deep charcoal pit.
Mmmmmm, GOOD!
And we eat gooey *poi* (POH-ee) paste with our fingers! Mmmmmm, GOOD!

Then we build a big bonfire and sing Christmas carols. I get to play my ukulele again. STRUM — STRUM — STRUM! I love Christmas in Hawaii!

Let's see if you can say "Merry Christmas" in Hawaiian.
"Mele Kalikimaka"
(MAY-lay kah-LEE-kee MAH-kah)
Can you say it? I'll bet you can.

HEY! Maybe you can come to Hawaii sometime and have a Christmas *luau* with us! I'd like that a lot!

Well, good-bye for now and Merry Christmas
from your friend Leilani
in **HAWAII!**

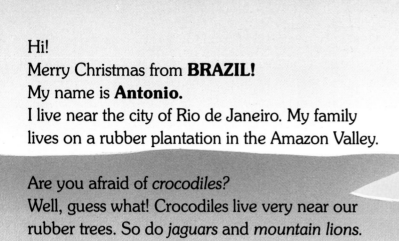

Hi!

Merry Christmas from **BRAZIL!**

My name is **Antonio.**

I live near the city of Rio de Janeiro. My family lives on a rubber plantation in the Amazon Valley.

Are you afraid of *crocodiles*?

Well, guess what! Crocodiles live very near our rubber trees. So do *jaguars* and *mountain lions.* So we are VERY careful!

I have a brother named Eugenio. Eugenio and I love to go boating and swimming. We can go all year around because the weather here is always HOT.

In Brazil, Christmas comes at the beginning of SUMMER VACATION! Can you believe *that!*

My favorite thing to do at Christmastime is to help set up the *presepio* (pre-SEP-ee-ooh). That's what we call a nativity scene. We set one up in the lobby of our hospital!

We start with life-size figures of Mary, Joseph, and baby Jesus. Then we stand up the figures of shepherds, sheep, cows, and camels. After that we add *sailboats* and *airplanes* and *tropical gardens,* and even an *electric train!*

Do you know why we do that?
We add these modern things
to the old ones to show the Christ child
all the NEW things we have learned
about since he was born.

On Christmas Eve, we wrap food and toys in white paper and ribbon. Then we take the gifts to church and lay them at the foot of baby Jesus in the *presepio* there. I am thankful I can share my food and toys with children who don't have as much as I do.
SHARING is an IMPORTANT thing to do!

The way we say "Merry Christmas"
in our language, Portuguese, is
"Feliz Natal."
(feh-LEES nah-TAHL)

Oh! I have to go now. Eugenio wants to go for a boat ride. Maybe we will see a *crocodile!*

Merry Christmas and good-bye
from your friend Antonio
in **BRAZIL!**

Hi!

Merry Christmas from the island of **SRI LANKA!**
My name is **Mali** (MA-lee). I live in the city of Kandy.
Isn't Kandy a *great* name for a city?

I have a sister named Sharmari (SHAR-mar-ee).
Sharmari and I do lots of things together. We talk to the
beautiful parrots that live in the coconut palms by our
house. (Sometimes, the parrots talk *back!*)

And we weave placemats for our mother out of reeds our
dad gathers by the river.

But one of our favorite things to do is to make paper
chains at Christmastime . . . GREEN and YELLOW
and BLUE and RED paper chains, like these:

We hang some of our paper chains
on our Christmas tree at home. And
we take some of our chains to church
to hang on the "Tree of Life." (That's
what we call the Christmas tree at
church!)

We help our mother make some
other decorations too — pretty
paper flowers, and big red bells,
and soft cotton snowflakes.
Aren't they BEAUTIFUL?

On Christmas morning, while it is still very dark, we light torches and join many people walking down our long hill to the Christmas sunrise service! We are very quiet. Then —

> Boom — BOOM — Boom!
> Drums beat in the distance.
> *Flash!* FLASH!
> Fireworks light up the sky.

Inside, the church is all dark except for the light from our burning torches. (THERE — can you see the bright paper chains we made?)

Everyone reads the wonderful Christmas story from the Bible out loud together — just as the sun peeks over the top of the hill.

Can you say "Merry Christmas" the way we do in our language, Tamil?

> **"Kirusmas Vazphuphal"**
> (KROOZ-ma FAR-too-dal)

Maybe you can make a beautiful PAPER CHAIN for your Christmas tree. I will tell you how in the back of this book. It's really easy and *fun*.
  I wish I could be there to do it with you!

> Merry Christmas and good-bye
> from your friend Mali
> in **SRI LANKA!**

Hi!
Merry Christmas from **NORWAY!**
My name is **Kjerste** (KEER-stee).
I live high in a mountain village called Otte (OO-te) in the country of Norway.

I have two brothers, Leif and Rolf. We love living in the mountains, but in the winter it gets cold, *cold,* COLD! We love to go sledding down the mountain and ice skating on the frozen ponds. And my whole family goes skiing through the green pine trees and around the crystal blue lakes.

Have *you* ever gone skiing through the pine trees or sledding down a mountain, really FAST?

HEY! Maybe you could come visit us in Norway sometime, and I will take you! It's *fun! Wheeeeeeeeeee!*

Christmas in Norway is *wonderful*. My favorite thing to do at Christmastime is to *dance around the Christmas tree!* We hold hands and dance in a circle around and around the tree while we sing our favorite Christmas songs. One of my uncles sings really loud, and sometimes he isn't exactly on the right note. But that's OK. We don't care!

Afterwards, we sit around the dining room table and eat my favorite dessert, creamy rice pudding called *grüd* (rhymes with *good*). *Grüd* is GOOD! It's covered with whipped cream. My mother hides a nut in one of the dishes of pudding, and whoever finds the nut wins a candy pig! Last year I won. I shared the candy pig with Leif and Rolf. *Mmmm*, GOOD!

If *you* want to make Norwegian rice pudding for *your* family this Christmas, I will give you the recipe at the back of this book!

Can you guess how we say "Merry Christmas" in Norwegian? Here it is.
"God Jul"
(good yool)
Isn't that *easy* to say?

I hope you have a very
"God Jul"!

Good-bye from your
friend Kjerste in
NORWAY!

Now, we want to know all about YOU. Fill in the blanks and add pictures to these two pages so we will know what YOU like to do at Christmastime!

PLACE
PHOTO
HERE

Hi!

My name is _Lily Maloney_.

I live in the city of _Baltimor_.

in the country of _USia land_

_____.

I like to _read_ and

do School.

Sometimes I _play with my Nabier_.

PLACE
PHOTO
HERE

I have _____ brothers and _1_ sisters.

We like to _Fight_ together.

My *favorite* thing to do at Christmastime is

Decorat the tree.

And sometimes we go on vacation

PLACE
PHOTO
HERE

The way we say "Merry Christmas" here is

(Meery) (chistmas)

PLACE
PHOTO
HERE

Good-bye and Merry Christmas

from your friend Lily maloney

in Baltimor !

Leilani

Antonio

Natasha

Mali

Pierre

Kanda

Samina

Yen-chi

Pablo

Merry Christmas, everyone!
Happy birthday, Jesus.
We *love* YOU!

Kjerste

Put YOUR name and picture here!
Join hands with us!

Hello from **Pablo** in Mexico!
Here is one way you can make a Mexican *piñata*.

1. Start with a **large brown paper grocery bag.**
   Decorate the bag with **paint, streamers, yarn,** and
   colored paper to look like an animal, a bird, or a star.

2. Fill the bag with **candy, nuts, fruit, popcorn,** and
   small toys.

3. Tie a **cord** or fasten a **strong rubber band** around the
   opening of the bag, like this:

4. Hang your wonderful *piñata* from a hook or broom
   handle, like this:

5. Blindfold one person at a time. Turn that person around
   once or twice. Let him or her try to hit the *piñata* with a
   wooden spoon or stick.

STAND BACK and *have fun!*

Good-bye now from your friend **Pablo!**

Hello from **Kjerste** in Norway!
Here is my recipe for my favorite Christmas pudding, *grüd*.

Good Grüd

1. Combine **2 quarts milk** and **1 cup regular rice** in top of double boiler. Cook slowly over low heat until thick — about 2 hours.

2. Add a pinch of salt and gently stir.

3. Cover and cool.

4. Carefully fold into rice mixture: **1 cup sugar** (or more to taste), **2 tablespoons vanilla**, and **2 cups whipped cream** (or whipped topping).

5. Spoon into individual dishes, cover, and chill. Be sure to hide an almond or walnut in one of the dishes!

Serve on Christmas Eve. Whoever finds the hidden nut wins a piece of candy!

I hope you like *grüd*.
I hope YOU find the nut!

Good-bye from your friend **Kjerste!**

Hello again from **Pierre** in France!
Here is how I make *beautiful* clay figures called *santons*.

1. First, I mix these three ingredients together very well:
   1 cup salt, 2 cups flour, and **1 cup water**.

   I add extra salt if needed
   until the dough is JUST RIGHT for modeling.

2. Then I make figures of the nativity — Mary, Joseph,
   baby Jesus (of course!), and all the animals. Once I
   made figures of *me* and my whole family!

3. Very carefully, I place the figures on a cookie sheet in
   the oven and BAKE them at 250° Fahrenheit until
   they are dry (1-2 hours, depending on size).

4. After the figures have cooled, I PAINT them *beautiful*
   colors with acrylic paints.

THERE THEY ARE!
Wasn't that *fun!*

Good-bye from your friend **Pierre!**

Hello! Do you remember me, **Mali** from Sri Lanka? Here is how I make *beautiful* paper chains!

1. I cut sheets of **different colored paper** into strips about 3/4" wide and 6"-8" long.

2. I **tape** the ends of one strip together to form a circle, like this:

3. Then I put a strip of a different color through that circle and tape the ends together to form another circle, like this:

4. Repeat for *every* paper strip. You can use as many paper strips as you want.

Use your beautiful paper Christmas CHAIN to decorate your *tree,* or a *window,* or your *room.*

How long can you make *your* chain? HAVE FUN!

Good-bye from your friend **Mali!**

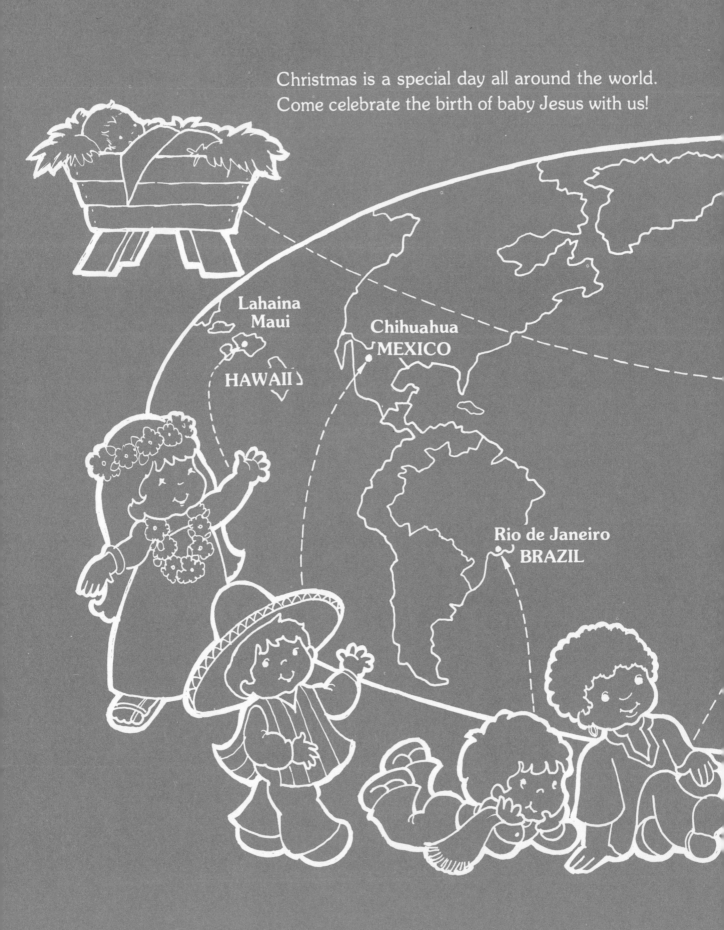

Christmas is a special day all around the world.
Come celebrate the birth of baby Jesus with us!

Lahaina
Maui

Chihuahua
MEXICO

HAWAII

Rio de Janeiro
BRAZIL